JAN   2014

LET'S EXPLORE THE

SOUTHEAST

BY KATHLEEN CONNORS

Gareth Stevens
Publishing

Please visit our website, www.garethstevens.com. For a free color catalog of all our high-quality books, call toll free 1-800-542-2595 or fax 1-877-542-2596.

Library of Congress Cataloging-in-Publication Data

Connors, Kathleen.
  Let's explore the Southeast / Kathleen Connors.
      pages cm. — (Road trip: exploring America's regions)
  Includes index.
  ISBN 978-1-4339-9145-5 (pbk.)
  ISBN 978-1-4339-9146-2 (6-pack)
  ISBN 978-1-4339-9144-8 (library binding)
  1. Southern States—Juvenile literature. I. Title. II. Title: Let us explore the Southeast.
  F209.3.C66 2013
  917.504'44—dc23

                                      2012049208

First Edition

Published in 2014 by
Gareth Stevens Publishing
111 East 14th Street, Suite 349
New York, NY 10003

Copyright © 2014 Gareth Stevens Publishing

Designer: Andrea Davison-Bartolotta
Editor: Kristen Rajczak

Photo credits: Cover, p. 1 (left) Jesse Kunerth/Shutterstock.com, (right), p. 9 (inset) Dave Allen Photography/Shutterstock.com; cover, back cover, interior backgrounds (texture) Marilyn Volan/Shutterstock.com; cover, back cover (map) Stacey Lynne Payne/Shutterstock.com; cover, back cover, pp. 1, 22–24 (green sign) Shutterstock.com; interior backgrounds (road) Renata Novackova/Shutterstock.com, (blue sign) Vitezslav Valka/Shutterstock.com; pp. 4, 5 (map), 7 (state outline), 21 iStockphoto/Thinkstock; p. 5 (curled corner) JonnyDrake/Shutterstock.com, (background) Darryl Vest/Shutterstock.com; p. 7 (background map) AridOcean/Shutterstock.com; pp. 9 (main), 17 (both insets, yellow note) iStockphoto/Thinkstock; p. 11 bartuchna@yahoo.pl/Shutterstock.com; p. 13 Murray Lee/age fotostock/Getty Images; p. 14 Bob Stefko/The Image Bank/Getty Images; p. 15 Brendan Smialowski/Getty Images; p. 17 (background) Blazej Lyjak/Shutterstock.com; p. 19 (map) courtesy of the National Park Service, (background) Phil Schermeister/National Geographic/Getty Images; p. 20 stocklight/Shutterstock.com; p. 21 (notebook) 89studio/Shutterstock.com.

Printed in the United States of America

CPSIA compliance information: Batch #CS13GS: For further information contact Gareth Stevens, New York, New York at 1-800-542-2595.

Contents

Words in the glossary appear in **bold** type the first time they are used in the text.

A Growing Region

The Southeast **region** of the United States is big—and its population grows every year. The 2010 census showed more than 85 million people lived there! You can see the 14 states most commonly included in the Southeast listed on the chart on the next page.

Taking a road trip through the Southeast would be exciting! Humming with people and events, cities like Atlanta, Georgia, and New Orleans, Louisiana, are fun to visit. Or you can explore the scenic mountain views of Kentucky and West Virginia.

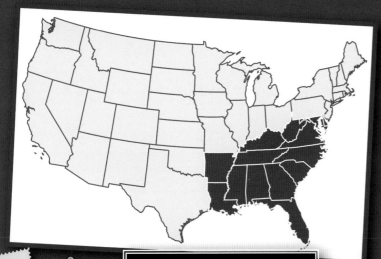

The Southeast

Washington, DC, is also found in the Southeast. It's not a state, but since it's the US capital and more than 600,000 people live there, it's an important part of the region.

The Southeast
at a Glance

	State	Population (2010)	Date of Statehood	Capital	State Bird	State Flower
1	Alabama	4,779,736	Dec. 14, 1819	Montgomery	yellowhammer and wild turkey	camellia and oak-leaf hydrangea
2	Arkansas	2,915,918	June 15, 1836	Little Rock	northern mockingbird	apple blossom
3	Delaware	897,934	Dec. 7, 1787	Dover	blue hen chicken	peach blossom
4	Florida	18,801,310	March 3, 1845	Tallahassee	northern mockingbird	orange blossom and coreopsis
5	Georgia	9,687,653	Jan. 2, 1788	Atlanta	brown thrasher	Cherokee rose and azalea
6	Kentucky	4,339,367	June 1, 1792	Frankfort	northern cardinal	goldenrod
7	Louisiana	4,533,372	April 30, 1812	Baton Rouge	eastern brown pelican	southern magnolia and Louisiana iris
8	Maryland	5,773,552	April 28, 1788	Annapolis	Baltimore oriole	black-eyed Susan
9	Mississippi	2,967,297	Dec. 10, 1817	Jackson	northern mockingbird and wood duck	southern magnolia
10	North Carolina	9,535,483	Nov. 21, 1789	Raleigh	northern cardinal	flowering dogwood
11	South Carolina	4,625,364	May 23, 1788	Columbia	Carolina wren	yellow Jessamine and Canada goldenrod
12	Tennessee	6,346,105	June 1, 1796	Nashville	northern mockingbird and bobwhite quail	iris and passionflower
13	Virginia	8,001,024	June 25, 1788	Richmond	northern cardinal	American dogwood
14	West Virginia	1,852,994	June 20, 1863	Charleston	northern cardinal	rhododendron

Bounded by Water

Have you ever been to the Outer Banks of North Carolina? Miami, Florida, is another common beachgoers' **destination**. The southeastern United States is bordered by the Atlantic Ocean in the east and the Gulf of Mexico in the south. That means there are lots of beaches!

Many other important bodies of water are found in the Southeast. The lower Mississippi River flows through Louisiana, Arkansas, Mississippi, Tennesee, and Kentucky. Maryland and Virginia create the bounds of Chesapeake Bay.

Pit Stop

Other large rivers in the Southeast, including the James, the Potomac, and the York Rivers, flow into Chesapeake Bay. Baltimore, Maryland, and Hampton Roads, Virginia, are just a few of the many cities found on these rivers.

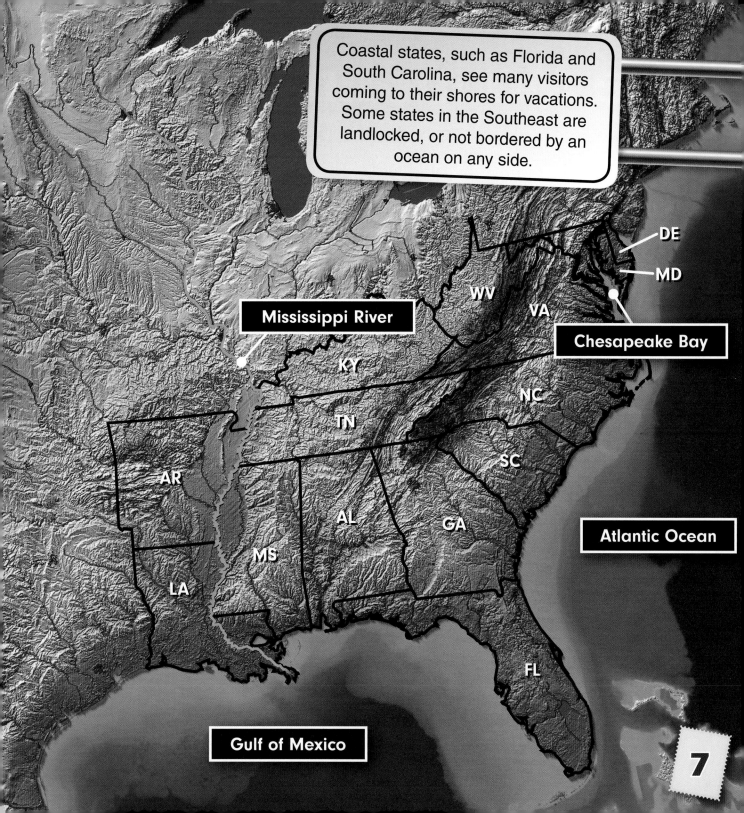

Coastal states, such as Florida and South Carolina, see many visitors coming to their shores for vacations. Some states in the Southeast are landlocked, or not bordered by an ocean on any side.

DE

MD

WV

VA

Mississippi River

Chesapeake Bay

KY

NC

TN

SC

AR

AL

GA

Atlantic Ocean

MS

LA

FL

Gulf of Mexico

The Mountains' Range

The Appalachian Mountains offer some of the best hiking, camping, and wildlife watching in the country—and this range is found throughout the Southeast! The Appalachians include the Alleghenies in West Virginia and Virginia, and the Blue Ridge Mountains found in Virginia and parts of North Carolina, South Carolina, and Georgia, among others.

Blue Ridge Parkway is a popular **route** for southeastern Appalachian road trips. It runs 469 miles (755 km) between Shenandoah National Park in Virginia and Great Smoky Mountains National Park in Tennessee.

Pit Stop

Crater of Diamonds State Park in Arkansas lets you dig for real diamonds—and the park says, "finders, keepers"!

Many national parks showcase the natural wonders of the southeastern Appalachian Mountains.

Blue Ridge Parkway

Some Like It Hot

The Gulf of Mexico, Atlantic Ocean, and Appalachian Mountains all play a part in the climate of states in the Southeast. States with coastal areas, such as Georgia, commonly have warm temperatures year-round. The mountains block cool air, while the Atlantic **Gulf Stream** brings in warm air.

Inland, summers can be hot. Alabama sometimes has temperatures nearing 100°F (38°C) during this season. Higher in the mountains, temperatures are lower. During winter, the northernmost states in the region may even have snow!

Pit Stop

Visitors to the Southeast should be mindful of **hurricane** season, which is June to November. This region sees the most hurricanes of any region in the United States.

Tourism is a big industry in the Southeast. From northerners trying to escape a cold winter to **anglers** hoping to catch a big fish, almost 10 million people visit the Southeast each year.

11

Jacksonville and Memphis

From the first colonial town of Jamestown, Virginia, to centers of the **civil rights movement**, cities in the southeast are full of history. The region's most populous city—Jacksonville, Florida—was settled in 1822. It's named after President Andrew Jackson, who was the area's governor for a short time.

The third-largest city in the Southeast is Memphis, Tennessee. The birthplace of blues music, Memphis's Beale Street draws crowds from all over the country, especially during its big music festival!

Pit Stop

Historic Rosedale Plantation in Charlotte shows what life was like in North Carolina during the 1800s. It was built in 1815 and was once home to slaves, as was common during that time in the South.

Post

Memphis is home to almost 650,000 people. Even more flood into the city during Memphis in May, a celebration of the city that includes a barbeque cooking contest!

13

The US Capital

The US president lives in Washington, DC! It's also home to some of the most famous places and buildings in the country. The White House, the National Archives—where the Declaration of Independence is kept—and many other places can be visited on a road trip through the Southeast.

In addition to historical sites, Washington, DC, has a rich arts community. The Kennedy Center, named for President John F. Kennedy, puts on some of the nation's best music and theater performances.

Pit Stop

Want to know what life was like in the **colonial** Southeast? Check out Colonial Williamsburg in Virginia! The town is set up as if it was the 18th century, and you can take a tour or even rent costumes and play along.

In honor of the great civil rights leader, the Martin Luther King Jr. Memorial in Washington, DC, opened in August 2011.

OUT OF THE MOUNTAIN OF DESPAIR, A STONE OF HOPE

Southern Hospitality

Food is a big part of the **culture** in the Southeast. From jambalaya in Louisiana to crab cakes in Maryland, this region's **cuisine** draws from the many groups that settled the region and local agriculture and seafood industries.

Soul food is made in a cooking style used by poor African Americans in the South after the Civil War. Today, most cities in the Southeast have plenty of restaurants that specialize in this kind of home cooking, including fried chicken, greens, sweet potatoes, okra, and cornbread.

Pit Stop

Post

Soul food was eaten in the Southeast for a long time before it was named during the civil rights movement in the 1960s.

Cornbread

Ingredients:

2 cups of coarse yellow cornmeal
3 tbsp flour
1 tsp baking powder
1 tsp baking soda
1 tsp salt
1 egg
2 cups buttermilk
2 tbsp bacon drippings or vegetable oil

There are so many recipes for cornbread in the Southeast. Some use a little flour, some use none at all. Most southern cornbread isn't sweet. This recipe is a simple, yummy cornbread. Ask an adult to help you make this southern food staple.

Directions:

1. Preheat the oven to 400 degrees. Put the bacon drippings or oil into a cast-iron skillet and put it in the oven until it sizzles.

2. In a bowl, mix the cornmeal, flour, baking powder, baking soda, and salt.

3. In another small bowl, whisk together the egg and buttermilk.

4. Add the dry ingredients to the egg and buttermilk. Mix well.

5. Take the cast-iron skillet out of the oven. Pour batter into it and place it back in the oven.

6. Bake for 20 to 25 minutes until light brown on the top.

7. Take the cornbread out of the oven and flip it over. Bake for an additional 5 minutes.

The Trail of Tears

To learn about the Native American cultures of the Southeast, tourists should be sure to visit the Trail of Tears National Historic Trail. Many Native American tribes once lived in the Southeast, including the Choctaw from Mississippi, Cherokees in North Carolina, and Seminoles in Florida. However, the Indian Removal Act of 1830 drove most of these tribes west.

The trail has starting points in Alabama, North Carolina, and Georgia. Visitors can follow several branches maintained in memory of the many who died on this journey.

Pit Stop

Chickamauga and Chattanooga National Military Park is found along the Trail of Tears. It was the location of an 1863 battle during the American Civil War when Northern states and Southern states fought each other.

During 1838 and 1839, southeastern Native American tribes were forced to move. You can follow one of the branches of the trail while on a road trip in the Southeast.

Trail
of
Tears

19

Well-Known Southerners

So many well-known people hail from states in the Southeast! Presidents Bill Clinton and Jimmy Carter were both from this region. You can visit Clinton's presidential library in Little Rock, Arkansas, and Carter's in Atlanta. Civil rights activist Rosa Parks was born in Tuskegee, Alabama. Both musician Louis Armstrong and writer Tennessee Williams lived in New Orleans.

Elvis was born in the Southeast, too! His home in Memphis, called Graceland, has become a road-trip destination for music lovers. Couples even get married there!

Bill Clinton

Weird and Wonderful Pit Stops in the Southeast

World's Longest Cave System
Mammoth Cave, Kentucky
There are 390 miles (628 km) of caves to explore at Mammoth Cave National Park.

Salt and Pepper Shaker Museum
Gatlinburg, Tennessee
See over 20,000 sets of salt and pepper shakers at this fun Tennessee stop!

Christmas, Florida
This holiday-named town has a Christmas tree up all year long. It's also home to the world's largest alligator-shaped building!

World's Largest Peanut Monument
Ashburn, Georgia
Though it's not the only big peanut in the United States, this monument is the largest.

Glossary

angler: a person who fishes for fun

civil rights movement: a time period in US history starting in the 1950s in which African Americans fought for equal civil rights, or the freedoms granted to us by law

colonial: having to do with the colonies, or land owned by another country

cuisine: a style of cooking

culture: the beliefs and ways of life of a group of people

destination: the place someone is traveling to

Gulf Stream: the warm current in the Atlantic Ocean that comes from the Gulf of Mexico and moves along the US coast

hurricane: a powerful storm that forms over water and causes heavy rainfall and high winds

region: an area

route: a path of travel

tourism: the business of drawing in tourists, or people traveling to visit another place

For More Information

Books

Hyde, Natalie. *What's in the Southeast?* New York, NY: Crabtree Publishing Company, 2012.

Marsico, Katie. *It's Cool to Learn About the United States. Southeast.* Ann Arbor, MI: Cherry Lake Publishing, 2012.

Websites

Landform Regions of the United States
www.eduplace.com/kids/socsci/books/applications/imaps/maps/g2_u2/index.html
Use this interactive map to learn where different landforms are in the regions of the United States.

Welcome to Kids' Capital
kids.dc.gov/kids_main_content.html
Learn more about the US capital city, located in the Southeast region, on this fun website. Play games and read lots of fun facts!

Index